# A Collection of Toccatas

BWV 910 BWV 911 BWV 912 BWV 913
BWV 914 BWV 915 BWV 916

By

Johann Sebastian Bach

For Solo Piano

Copyright © 2011 Read Books Ltd.
This book is copyright and may not be
reproduced or copied in any way without
the express permission of the publisher in writing

**British Library Cataloguing-in-Publication Data**
A catalogue record for this book is available from
the British Library

# Contents

Toccata in C minor BWV 911....................*Page 1*

Toccata in D Major BWV 912.................*Page 13*

Toccata in D minor BWV 913.................*Page 23*

Toccata in E minor BWV 914 .................*Page 34*

Toccata in F-sharp minor BWV 910......*Page 41*

Toccata in G Major BWV 916.................*Page 52*

Toccata in G minor BWV 915.................*Page 60*

# TOCCATA.

Adagio.

piano

B. W. III.

# V.
# TOCCATA.
### D-dur.

*Variante der nächsten zwölf Takte im Anhang I. No 3ª.

*Variante dieses Zwischensatzes im Anhang I. N? 3♭.

B.W. XXXVI.

# VI.
# TOCCATA.
### D-moll.

B. W. XXXVI.

B.W. XXXVI.

B. W. XXXVI.

B. W. XXXVI.

# VII.
# TOCCATA.
### E-moll.

B.W. XXXVI.

Fuga. (a 3 voci.)
Allegro.

B.W. XXXVI.

B.W. XXXVI.

B. W. XXXVI.

# TOCCATA.

Presto e staccato.

# IX.
## TOCCATA.
### G-dur.

B. W. XXXVI.

Allegro.

# VIII.
# TOCCATA.
G-moll.

B.W. XXXVI.

B.W. XXXVI.

www.ingramcontent.com/pod-product-compliance
Lightning Source LLC
Chambersburg PA
CBHW080640170426
43200CB00015B/2907